D1315882

AMAZING INVENTORS & INNOVATORS

THE WRIGHT BROTHERS

LYNN DAVIS

Consulting Editor, Diane Craig, M.A./Reading Specialist

Super Sandcastle

An Imprint of Abdo Publishing
abdopublishing.com

abdopublishing.com

Published by Abdo Publishing, a division of ABDO, PO Box 398166, Minneapolis, Minnesota 55439. Copyright © 2016 by Abdo Consulting Group, Inc. International copyrights reserved in all countries. No part of this book may be reproduced in any form without written permission from the publisher. Super SandCastle™ is a trademark and logo of Abdo Publishing.

Printed in the United States of America, North Mankato, Minnesota
062015
092015

Editor: Liz Salzmann
Content Developer: Nancy Tuminelly
Cover and Interior Design and Production: Mighty Media, Inc.
Photo Credits: Library of Congress, Shutterstock, Wikicommons

Library of Congress Cataloging-in-Publication Data

Davis, Lynn, 1981- author.
The Wright Brothers / Lynn Davis ; consulting editor, Diane Craig, M.A./Reading Specialist.
    pages cm. -- (Amazing inventors & innovators)

Audience: K to grade 4
ISBN 978-1-62403-726-9

1. Wright, Wilbur, 1867-1912--Juvenile literature. 2. Wright, Orville, 1871-1948--Juvenile literature. 3. Inventors--United States--Biography--Juvenile literature. 4. Aeronautics--United States--Biography--Juvenile literature. 5. Aeronautics--United States--History--Juvenile literature. I. Title.

TL540.W7D38 2016
629.13'0092'273--dc23
                    2014046602

Super SandCastle™ books are created by a team of professional educators, reading specialists, and content developers around five essential components—phonemic awareness, phonics, vocabulary, text comprehension, and fluency—to assist young readers as they develop reading skills and strategies and increase their general knowledge. All books are written, reviewed, and leveled for guided reading, early reading intervention, and Accelerated Reader™ programs for use in shared, guided, and independent reading and writing activities to support a balanced approach to literacy instruction.

CONTENTS

The Wright Brothers

The Early Years

Bicycle Beginnings

Just Wing It

Gliding to Victory

Steering Clear

Testing, Testing, One, Two, Three

The Engine that Could

First Flight

More About the Wright Brothers

Test Your Knowledge

Glossary

THE WRIGHT BROTHERS

Wilbur (left) and Orville (right) Wright as children

The Wright brothers' home in Ohio

The Wright brothers lived in Ohio. They were inventors. They built the first airplane.

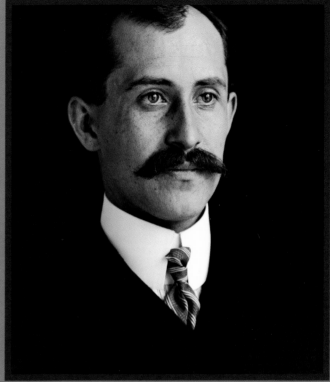

WILBUR WRIGHT

BORN: April 16, 1867, Millville, Indiana

DIED: May 30, 1912, Dayton, Ohio

MARRIAGE: never got married

CHILDREN: did not have any children

ORVILLE WRIGHT

BORN: August 19, 1871, Dayton, Ohio

DIED: January 30, 1948, Dayton, Ohio

MARRIAGE: never got married

CHILDREN: did not have any children

THE EARLY YEARS

The Wright brothers had other jobs first. They ran a printing shop. Then they started the Wright Cycle Company. They fixed bikes. They also built bikes.

Wilbur (left) and Orville (right) Wright in 1897

This was the Wright brothers' bicycle shop from 1895 to 1897.

THE WRIGHT CYCLE CO.

BICYCLE BEGINNINGS

The brothers knew a lot about bikes. This helped them make aircraft.

This was the Wright brothers' bicycle shop from 1897 to 1908.

One of five bicycles made by the Wright brothers that still exist

▲ Orville and Edwin Sines working in the bicycle shop

▲ Wilbur working in the bicycle shop

Augustus Herring testing a Herring-Chanute glider, 1896 ▼

They also studied other aircraft. They added to what other people did. This helped them make better aircraft.

JUST WING IT

Wilbur and Orville also studied how birds fly. Birds change the shape of their wings. That is how they **steer**.

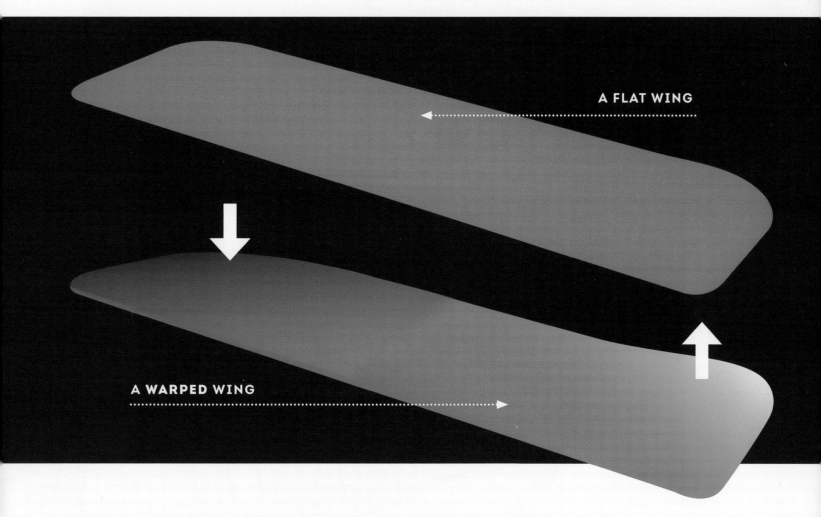

A FLAT WING

A WARPED WING

They thought aircraft could work the same way.
They made wings that could bend.

GLIDING TO VICTORY

The brothers tested their ideas with kites.
Then they built gliders.

Most people leaned their bodies to **steer** gliders.
Wilbur and Orville wanted to use the wings.

WHAT IS A GLIDER?

A glider is an aircraft. It has wings.
It does not have an engine.
It coasts on the wind.

STEERING CLEAR

The Wright brothers **steered** their glider in three ways.

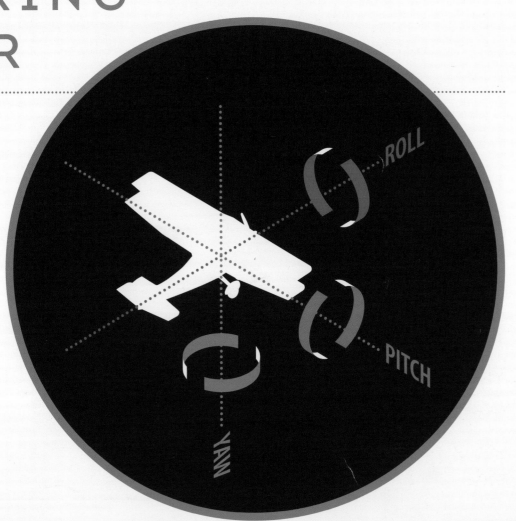

ROLL

PITCH

YAW

ROLL

They could tip the ends of the wings up and down.

PITCH

They could tip the body up and down.

YAW

They could move the body from side to side.

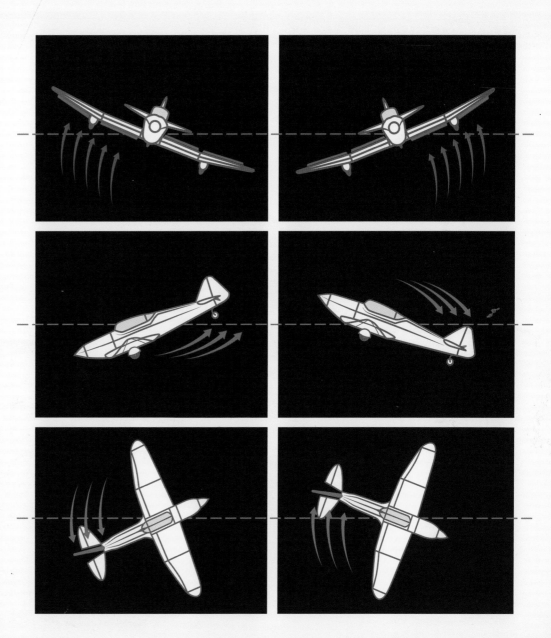

TESTING, TESTING, ONE, TWO, THREE

Wilbur and Orville made many test flights. They built better gliders. They tested many different wing shapes.

Finally they knew enough.
They were ready to build
a powered aircraft.

Kitty Hawk is in North Carolina. It is by the Atlantic Ocean. Wilbur and Orville tested their gliders on the beach. The Wright Brothers National Memorial is in Kitty Hawk.

The Wright Brothers
National Memorial

THE ENGINE THAT COULD

Wilbur and Orville built an engine for their airplane. It was very light.

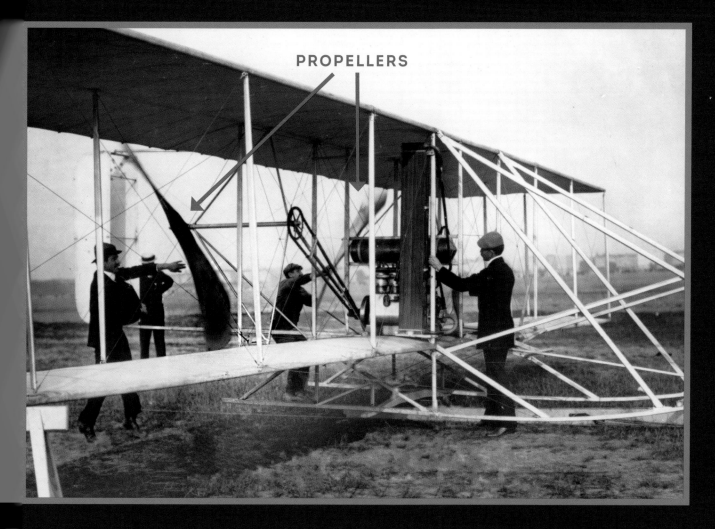

PROPELLERS

They added **propellers**. The blades were shaped like wings. They put all the parts together. They called it the Wright Flyer.

FIRST FLIGHT

The Wright Brothers flew their airplane at Kitty Hawk.

The first flight was on December 17, 1903.
Orville flew the plane. Wilbur ran beside it.

The first flight lasted only a few seconds. But that was long enough. The brothers had invented the airplane!

MORE ABOUT THE WRIGHT BROTHERS

Neither Wright brother finished HIGH SCHOOL.

Orville was very SHY. Wilbur did all the public speaking.

Wilbur and Orville both wanted to fly FIRST. They flipped a coin to decide.

TEST YOUR KNOWLEDGE

1. What did the Wright Brothers fix and make at the shop they owned?

2. Where did the Wright Brothers test their aircraft?

3. The Wright Brothers studied dolphins to help them make better aircraft. True or false?

THINK ABOUT IT!

How would you build a flying machine?

GLOSSARY

propeller - a device with turning blades used to move a vehicle such as an airplane or a boat.

steer - to control the direction a car, boat, or airplane travels in.

warp - to bend or twist.